At Issue

|Disaster Planning

Other Books in the At Issue Series:

At Issue

Disaster Planning

Janel Morris, Book Editor

GREENHAVEN PRESS
A part of Gale, Cengage Learning

GALE
CENGAGE Learning™

Detroit • New York • San Francisco • New Haven, Conn • Waterville, Maine • London

Christine Nasso, *Publisher*
Elizabeth Des Chenes, *Managing Editor*

For more information, contact:
Greenhaven Press
27500 Drake Rd.
Farmington Hills, MI 48331-3535
Or you can visit our Internet site at gale.cengage.com

Articles in Greenhaven Press anthologies are often edited for length to meet page requirements. In addition, original titles of these works are changed to clearly present the main thesis and to explicitly indicate the author's opinion. Every effort is made to ensure that Greenhaven Press accurately reflects the original intent of the authors. Every effort has been made to trace the owners of copyrighted material.

Cover photograph © Sue Poynton. Image from BigStockPhoto.com.

LIBRARY OF CONGRESS CATALOGING-IN-PUBLICATION DATA

Disaster planning / Janel Morris, book editor.
  p. cm. -- (At issue)
  Includes bibliographical references and index.
  ISBN 978-0-7377-4090-5 (hardcover)
  ISBN 978-0-7377-4091-2 (pbk.)
  1. Disaster relief--United States--Planning. 2. Emergency management--United States.I. Morris, Janel.
  HV555.U6D58 2009
  363.34'520973--dc22

                                                              2008028545

Printed in the United States of America
1 2 3 4 5 6 7 12 11 10 09 08

Contents

Introduction

From the Pacific to the Atlantic coast, the United States has seen its share of natural disasters. Earthquakes eat away at the California coastline while fires devour the state's homes and natural resources; tornadoes leave paths of destruction through the central states and hurricanes ravage the Gulf. Technology of the modern era has increased the risk of man-made disasters; nuclear warfare capabilities threaten to take more lives in a single strike than at any other time in history. The United States is a nation on constant alert for the next catastrophe, but many question how well-prepared it is to survive a disaster with minimal loss and make a swift recovery.

Since the terrorist attacks on September 11, 2001, many advances have been made in national security. Despite this, polls indicate Americans generally do not feel any more protected from terrorism, and many believe the government is not doing all it can to ensure public safety. Changes in security and disaster recovery are made each time the existing system fails, but what improvements are made to prevent serious injury and death before disaster strikes? The 2007 collapse of the Interstate 35W bridge in Minneapolis could have been prevented had authorities responded to warnings about weaknesses in the bridge's integrity, reported ten years before it gave way and sent more than 50 vehicles into the Mississippi River. Why did Minnesota officials not learn from the tragic error Louisiana authorities made in failing to repair unstable levees which failed during Hurricane Katrina and caused needless death and destruction?

Perhaps the greatest debate when it comes to preparing for and recovering from disasters is, Who is responsible? Is it the federal government? State and local authorities? Individual citizens? This issue came to a head during Hurricane Katrina. The city of New Orleans seemed grossly unprepared for the

destruction the 2005 storm brought, and in the days following, newspapers and television stations provided constant coverage of an overcrowded Superdome with no plumbing, senior citizens baking in the August sun with no way to keep
their medications refrigerated, and hundreds of victims
stranded on rooftops, waist-deep in water, or waiting on high-
way shoulders.

Who was at fault for the loss of life and property, and for
failing to render swift aid to the survivors? Fingers pointed in
every direction. The Army Corps of Engineers was blamed for
not repairing structurally unsound levees which broke and
flooded the 9th Ward district during the hurricane. President
George W. Bush and the Federal Emergency Management
Agency were accused of delaying and bumbling federal assistance. New Orleans mayor Ray Nagin was denounced for failing to utilize several hundred school buses to evacuate city
residents without personal transportation, leading to unnecessary deaths. The governor of Louisiana was criticized for not
preparing for such an emergency in an area where hurricane
destruction is frequent. New Orleans residents themselves received sharp rebuke from Mississippi citizens (also hit by Hurricane Katrina) for failing to pull themselves up by their own
bootstraps. It remains to be seen whether anyone will learn
from the mistakes made in 2005 in order to better equip citizens to survive the next hurricane.

The national, state, and local response to wildfires that
ravaged southern California in 2007 demonstrated some evi-
dence that authorities learned from the past. Mistakes made
during previous firestorms and during Hurricane Katrina
were corrected as evacuations were carried out without panic,
shelters were easily accessible and well-stocked, and the governor and President met with victims and evaluated situations
personally.

Advances in technology, communications, preparation,
and rescue efforts can never completely eliminate the negative

consequences of disaster. But individuals, communities, companies, and governments all stand to gain from disaster planning, an activity best undertaken precisely when its benefits are not needed. These are the type of situations examined in *At Issue: Disaster Planning.*

1

Businesses Strive to Make Changes After Hurricane Katrina

Bridget Mintz Testa

Bridget Mintz Testa is a writer based in Houston.

For businesses in the New Orleans area, Hurricane Katrina was a wake-up call for employers to develop solutions for disaster-related crises, including delivery of payroll, decentralizing head-quarters, and finding housing for displaced employees. Even companies trained to deal with emergency situations found ways to make improvements as a result of the 2005 disaster.

Despite the difficulties of life in New Orleans one year after Hurricane Katrina, business is returning to normal for many organizations. That doesn't mean things are the same as they were before.

The catastrophic hurricane, which caused $135 billion in damage as it roared through Louisiana and Mississippi in late August 2005, marked a permanent shift in the region's business and workforce operations.

Employers such as Sodexho, State Farm, Entergy and Tulane University struggled with common post-hurricane issues for their workers. They had to find emergency and temporary housing, provide financial assistance, extend health insurance and other benefits beyond the usual sign-up dates, relocate personnel and put people back to work.

These organizations, and quite possibly every business and institution in the city, have documented the lessons learned and are developing plans for the future so they won't be unprepared should another catastrophe hit. For Sodexho and State Farm, the effort closely follows disaster planning, whereas Entergy and Tulane have made more structural business changes.

Finding and Paying Employees

Immediately after Katrina, food and facility services provider Sodexho faced its biggest challenge: finding its 1,400 widely scattered New Orleans employees. The company went to great lengths to locate them, bringing in personnel from unaffected states to look for workers at their homes. They also assembled teams to make phone calls and rented a plane with a banner bearing Sodexho contact information to fly over the Houston Astrodome, where thousands of people from New Orleans had been relocated in the weeks after Katrina. It also set up an 800 number so employees could access information and leave their contact numbers and addresses.

Once Sodexho located employees, its next challenge was paying them. "The majority of our New Orleans employees are food service workers, housekeepers, porters and utility workers," says Sharon Matthews, senior director of corporate human resources. "They're an hourly wage population, and they live paycheck to paycheck."

The solution: "We wired money to hundreds of locations," Matthews says.

Finding and paying 1,400 employees in a crisis spurred Sodexho to develop a new employee tracking system.

[A year later], 70 percent of Sodexho's New Orleans employees are back on the job in the city. The other 30 percent either quit or never contacted the company and were terminated on December 31. The company hired replacements for them, and its 75 primarily educational and hospital services accounts in the city are up and running.

Finding and paying 1,400 employees in a crisis spurred Sodexho to develop a new employee tracking system. Employee location data had to be input manually into a spreadsheet after Katrina, but the new system is Web-based. The 800 contact number established during Katrina has become the company's lone disaster number. "We also now ask employees to regularly update their contact information," Matthews says. "We want not only their numbers in New Orleans, but elsewhere too."

Wire transfer remains the best emergency method for Sodexho to pay its hourly employees, who are most comfortable with their weekly paper checks. "We have done a big campaign on direct deposit," Matthews says, "but we don't try to force employees to do anything."

Sodexho is also looking for a way for employees to take company information with them in the event of another disaster. It hasn't quite settled on the final form, but the content will include what to do, whom to contact at the company and how to do it, and the information the company will need from the employee. Sodexho has also established an executive team whose members will make emergency decisions. It's proactively contemplating disasters that could be worse than Katrina. "There is already a task force working on avian flu," Matthews says.

Personnel Reserves

For insurer State Farm, dealing with disaster is core to its business. It's not surprising that the company has a specially trained catastrophe services force of 2,600 employees ready to travel to stricken areas within 24 hours and stay for as long as six months to handle claims.

Independent adjusting firms, with whom State Farm has contracts, assist the first line of defense by dispatching adjusters to ease the workload.

Expanding the number of adjusters requested from independent firms and using its operations center technology to handle claims virtually are two methods State Farm has added to its arsenal of emergency plans.

"After Katrina, we had a shortage of resources, even with our catastrophe services people," says Morris Anderson, a spokesman for the company. State Farm called on its independent adjusters, asking for additional help beyond the contracted numbers. "As an example, whereas we may typically have had 150 adjusters committed from a particular company, we may have asked them for 50 more," Anderson says.

Ultimately, 2,750 to 3,500 independents were called in to handle claims in Louisiana, in addition to the 2,600 catastrophe services employees. Today, about 100 to 150 State Farm employees remain in Louisiana, handling claims from Katrina and Hurricane Rita, which devastated the region just three weeks later, causing an estimated $10 billion in damage.

Expanding the number of adjusters requested from independent firms and using its operations center technology to handle claims virtually are two methods State Farm has added to its arsenal of emergency plans. It's also trying to establish a bigger pool of temporary clerical employees who could help with the paperwork that would follow another Katrina-size crisis. "It was a big challenge to get enough people [to Louisiana]," Anderson says.

Decentralizing Headquarters

Energy company Entergy's corporate headquarters staff of 1,500 was housed in two buildings in downtown New Orleans when Katrina struck. Afterward, corporate headquarters was temporarily moved to Jackson, Mississippi.

"Our challenge was finding housing on the fly for 1,500 employees," spokesman Morgan Stewart says. Entergy responded by paying for housing for employees from October 1 through July 31. By the end of that period, the 1,000 employees whose homes were destroyed or otherwise rendered uninhabitable had been able to file claims and find new lodging.

Entergy also created the Power of Hope Fund, which raised $4.2 million through donations from employees, the industry and the company. The funds were distributed to employees through more than 4,000 grants averaging $1,000 each. Operation Restore Hope brought in donations of furniture, clothes, cleaning supplies and other necessities throughout Entergy's operating region of Arkansas, Louisiana, Mississippi and Texas. Employees took what they needed, and the rest went to the Red Cross.

The experiences were incorporated into Entergy's new business continuity plan, which was created "to deal with the storm but also any catastrophes in the future," Stewart says.

"We learned how to redeploy and provide housing and furniture for employees," Stewart says. "We did that on the fly after Katrina, and we're now solidifying that as part of the planning process. We also learned that corporate employees didn't all have to be in the same place. We could distribute them."

The knowledge that corporate headquarters and its staff could be decentralized came in handy when the company moved its headquarters back to New Orleans in April. One of the two buildings it had previously occupied was ruined, so employees were shifted to other locations. "The majority are back in New Orleans, but there are operations that have moved," Stewart says. "We've established primary offices in Hammond, Louisiana; Little Rock, Arkansas; and Jackson, Mississippi."

Corporate employees associated with those operations have moved with them. Hammond will host back-office functions. Little Rock will become the company's information technology center, in addition to serving in its original role as the company's Arkansas headquarters. Jackson was already the company's Mississippi headquarters and home to its nuclear power operations. Now it will also handle energy transmission functions. The Woodlands, near Houston, had been home to system planning and fossil fuel operations. Now it will add some financial operations.

A University's Struggles

Tulane University, the largest private employer in New Orleans, sustained $400 million in losses, including $160 million in property damage, and the school closed for the fall 2005 semester. Of the 110 buildings spread across the university's two city campuses, 85 were damaged by wind and flooding. Ultimately, only two buildings were irremediably ruined, but repairing and renovating the others was costly.

While nearly all faculty and professional staff returned to the university when it reopened in January [2006], there's still a severe shortage of skilled and unskilled workers to handle duties such as plant operations and maintenance, electrical needs, security, day care and custodial work. "We're struggling to meet mandatory plant-operations personnel requirements," says Anthony Lorino, CFO and senior vice president of operations for the university.

Tulane has increased wages to better compete for trade employees in a city where hourly workers appear to be in shorter supply than professionals are. The university has also expanded job advertising to local television, print ads and billboards, in addition to ads on the school's Web site.

2

Lessons from September 11 Lead to Better Emergency Communication

Joab Jackson

Joab Jackson is a staff writer for Government Computer News.

In an age of instant information and media frenzy, local and national governments must find the most effective way to notify citizens in case of an emergency. City-wide sirens and television emergency broadcast systems are useful, but after the events of September 11, 2001, the Homeland Security Department must find new ways to deliver warnings and recovery instructions with more efficiency than the established systems.

In the golden days of broadcasting, alerting the populace to an impending disaster was easy. With only three major television networks, and a limited number of radio stations, the government could simply send an electronic warning to those media outlets, which would relay the message to their audiences. Everyone of a certain age remembers the tests of the emergency broadcast system.

But the conduits of communications have multiplied exponentially. People watching television could be tuned in to any one of hundreds of channels. They could be visiting one of millions of Web sites, or communicating via cell phones, pagers or chat rooms. How can the government alert the populace to, for instance, a terrorist attack?

Joab Jackson, "Next Steps for Technology," *Government Computer News*, September 11, 2006. http://gcn.com. Reproduced by permission.

This was one of the many technology challenges the country had to face after Sept. 11, 2001. Changing threats demand new capabilities, and government, along with industry, poured money into fresh technology initiatives.

The events of Sept. 11 "changed the dynamics of what we need to do," said Ann Buckingham, deputy director of the Federal Emergency Management Agency's Office of National Security Coordination.

"We have entered into a period over these past five years that has been almost totally unlike anything we have been through in the past," said Jules Duga, a senior researcher at Battelle Memorial Institute of Columbus, Ohio. Among other things, Battelle runs several labs for the Energy Department.

Duga compiles an annual report on R&D spending in both the private and public sectors. While federal spending has grown modestly in the last five years, the shift of funds to counterterrorism work has been noticeable. "There has been a concentration of funding in detection and amelioration of potential impacts of terrorist attacks," Duga said. "There's [also] been a lot that went into prevention by enhancing technologies for surveillance and intelligence."

You don't want to be dependent on people watching TV or having their radio on all the time.

Five years later, several new technology initiatives are beginning to bear fruit.

Digital Alert System

When a terrorist attack or natural disaster occurs, warning citizens is the job of the Emergency Alert System, now overseen by the Homeland Security Department. For decades, it was on stand-by, waiting to send audio alert messages to television networks and, by relay, to radio stations.

"You don't want to be dependent on people watching TV or having their radio on all the time," Buckingham said.

FEMA is working to create a set of technologies, called the Integrated Public Alert and Warning System [IPAWS], that can render an alert message to additional forms of media. IPAWS would send out warnings via cell phones, cable television, satellite radio, pagers, the Internet and other new media.

One of the chief components of IPAWS is the Digital Emergency Alert System [DEAS], which when fully deployed will be able to send emergency video, audio, text messages and even file attachments across the country within minutes, said Kevin Briggs, readiness division director for FEMA.

Initially, DEAS messages will be sent over the sub-bands of the PBS television channels, allowing other media outlets to grab the warnings with a simple receiver for rebroadcast on their own channels. The new digital channels allow multiple sub-bands for each channel. PBS donated to FEMA one channel, which can carry up to 1 Mbps—enough for text and file transfers.

In 2004, FEMA set up a prototype with WETA, a PBS station near Washington, D.C. It is now setting up national coverage through the PBS satellite backbone. Currently, DEAS covers 17 states and will be rolled out nationwide by the end of 2007. The pilot cost $1 million, Briggs said, and the whole program would cost $4.5 million to deploy and $1 million a year to maintain. Although this approach could reach 99 percent of the U.S. population, FEMA plans to establish other conduits as well. The agency is speaking with cellular phone companies about the possibility of sending out bulk alert messages, which cell and land-line phone users could subscribe to. Such messages could be localized to specific regions by mapping them to certain cell phone towers.

3

The U.S. Army Prepares for Disasters on the Homefront

Patti Bielling

Patti Bielling works for the U.S. Army, North, Public Affairs Office.

Army North, created in October 2005, comprises 500 soldiers and civilians prepared to assist civil authorities in response to natural disasters on U.S. soil. Though few know about the command and its mission, this military unit has been critical in disaster recovery during wildfires and hurricanes since its inception.

When a hurricane barrels toward the United States or wild fires threaten, U.S. Army, North, is prepared to assist civil authorities in the response.

Created in October 2005, Army North is the Army component of U.S. Northern Command, the unified command responsible for homeland defense and support of civil authorities.

The more than 500 soldiers and civilians of Army North maintain their readiness through robust planning, realistic training, and established relationships with critical civilian and military partners in homeland defense and consequence management.

Not many people know about the new command and its mission, said Col. Jeffrey Buchanan, Army North's director of operations.

Patti Bielling, "Preparing for Disaster," *Soldiers Magazine*, vol. 62, no. 6, June 2007, pp. 38–41.

"This is now a full-time job," Col. Buchanan said. "When a disaster happens, it's not a pick-up team. We work with our state federal partners every day, and that will help make the federal government and the Department of Defense [DOD] response more effective."

Soldiers and Firefighters

During the 2006 wildfire season, for example, Army North oversaw a battalion of 500 soldiers who worked side by side with civilian firefighters to battle the Tripod Complex fire in north-central Washington.

The military's contribution was critical in a busy fire season in which more than 9 million acres burned, said Doug Shinn of the National Interagency Fire Center in Boise, Idaho, the federal organization responsible for committing the nation's fire-management resources.

"Deploying a military battalion allowed us to diversify our assets," Mr. Shinn said. "We were able to reallocate civilian crews to fight other large fires and to conduct initial attacks on fires throughout the West."

In the end, the soldiers helped protect about 500 structures near Mazama, Wash. They helped battle the flames and constructed more than 50 miles of fire lines to contain the Tripod Complex fire.

Preparing for Cooperation

When a hurricane or other disaster overwhelms state resources, Army North is also prepared to assist, Buchanan said.

"If a state requests federal assistance, DOD may be employed as part of the federal response package, bringing additional capabilities to save lives and restore life-support systems," Col. Buchanan said. "We could be asked to do such things as search and rescue, distribute food and supplies, provide clean water or safe shelter, restore communications or provide medical support."

Ardent Sentry '07 was the latest exercise designed to test Army North's ability to respond to multiple disasters, including a simulated hurricane striking New England, and terrorist attacks in the Midwest and Alaska. The exercise was sponsored in early May by the Department of Homeland Security, Federal Emergency Management Agency and the Department of Defense.

Army North's homeland-defense mission includes deterring, detecting, preventing and defeating attacks on the United States or its citizens.

"Training events like this allow federal, state and local agencies to review processes and techniques and build relationships," said Army North exercise planner LTC Paul Condon. "It was designed to be challenging and complex, so agencies can stress their people and resources and look at new options and solutions."

Army North deployed one of its two operational command posts to the Northeast to exercise command and control processes for national forces responding to the hurricane. With augmentation, these scalable organizations may expand to joint task forces, and the headquarters at Army North can organize as a joint task force, command and control multiple joint task forces, or can expand into a joint force land component command.

An Able Team

Other key players during a disaster are Army North's 10 Defense Coordinating Officers [DCOs], who are DOD representatives on the ground to coordinate use of military resources with federal and state authorities. These officers and a small staff are collocated with each of the Federal Emergency Management Agency regional headquarters, and strive to become experts on state and federal response plans.

Maj. John D. Ring is the operations officer for Region III, which includes West Virginia, Virginia, Pennsylvania, Delaware, Maryland and the District of Columbia. He said he has attended a number of consequence-management events in the last year.

"Participating in those conferences and exercises gives us a chance to coordinate with planners and responders before something happens," Maj. Ring said. "We've also gained an appreciation for the states' capabilities—I'm very impressed with what they can do."

The DCOs also interface with military installations within their regions that may be designated as support platforms during a contingency.

Maj. Ring said the job is like nothing he's ever done before.

"There was a steep learning curve—a whole new language and a whole new set of rules to learn," he said. "We in the Army are trained to go in and take charge, but during a civil-support mission, we really are in a support role, so it's a different way of doing business. I love the challenge." . . .

Army North's homeland-defense mission includes deterring, detecting, preventing and defeating attacks on the United States or its citizens, said Col. Jeffrey Buchanan, Army North's director of operations. "That could range anywhere from a terrorist attack to a missile launch targeting the United States to an enemy army coming across the nation's borders," he said.

Army North conducts conferences and training activities with the Mexican and Canadian armies. "The overarching goal is to develop an enhanced partnership that will lead to a higher level of security for all North Americans," said Maj. John Hytten, foreign area officer for the command.

4

Schools Must Protect Students by Planning for Emergencies

Michael Dorn

Michael Dorn is the executive director of Safe Havens, International, Inc., a nonprofit school safety organization.

With a dramatic rise in school shootings over the past decade and an increased risk of terrorist attacks, school administrators should make disaster preparation a priority. However, the security of schools across the nation is inconsistent and many students are in danger of serious injury or death that could be prevented with a little planning.

The contrast between safety in schools and school systems astounds me. We recently worked with schools in the Asheville, NC region who have been steadfastly improving their safety program from the past two years. A four district regional collaborative has conducted hundreds of training sessions, planning meetings, consulting sessions and drills and exercises to enhance the level of emergency preparedness for all four participating districts. The districts are developing a series of advanced but concise customized training DVD's and video crisis scenarios to more effectively educate and prepare school employees. The districts are printing revised emergency reference charts for different categories of employees such as administrators, teachers, school bus drivers and custodians that are integrated, yet specific to different job roles. During

Michael Dorn, "Alert or Asleep at the Wheel," *Doors and Hardware*, vol. 71, no. 12, December 2007, pp. 39–40. Copyright © 2007 Door and Hardware Institute. Reproduced by permission.

the project, a major hazardous materials event threatened the safety of thousands of students and staff. The incident was handled almost flawlessly by well-prepared school and public safety officials. The long-term and effective efforts by these four districts have required a level of commitment above that of most school systems in the United States and abroad. However, the results have proven to be well worth the investment in time and money.

About this time, a multiple-victim school shooting took place in another school district, demonstrating some pretty serious gaps in the district's level of safety and emergency preparedness. A district administrator was contacted by multiple students with concerns about the student prior to the incident and it is clear the best practice of multi-disciplinary threat assessment was not utilized. The district was still reliant upon the use of code phrases to signal emergency situations and, as has happened on numerous occasions around the nation, many staff and students misunderstood the codes and did not understand what they were supposed to do. The use of codes to signal lockdowns, and other emergency functions is a pretty well known planning flaw because the concept has failed so many times before. The United States Department of Education and the Federal Emergency Management Agency have been advising schools not to use codes for this reason for some time now. After this incident, students, parents and even school employees have appeared in the national media criticizing the lack of safety measures at the school where the shooting took place.

A Matter of Life and Death

Having worked with more than 2,000 public and independent schools and school districts worldwide, we are impressed with how much effort goes into safety at some schools and shocked at how little is in place at others. Clearly some school educational organizations are alert and vigilant while others are not so focused on safety. Most educational organizations lie somewhere between these two extremes. You did not hear about the first school district in the media because the potential tragedy they faced was averted by their vigilance. Each day, students continue to learn there instead of being continually distracted by the tragedy that could have easily struck had school officials not been so focused on safety. Conversely, the school shooting mentioned above is a good example of why making safety must be a priority. The district will now assuredly face considerable civil liability, staff and students have been injured and many more emotionally traumatized, key school officials will spend thousands of hours trying to respond to the incident, public confidence has been severely shaken and the process of education has come to a screeching halt. Sadly, many educational organizations have found themselves in this predicament with immeasurable damage to people and the very process of education.

Driven by well-meaning government initiatives, the obsession with test scores has become so all encompassing that many educators push other critical issues like safety aside.

Of course, many readers . . . know this is not unique to emergency preparedness measures. It is just as common to see schools with no viable access control system in place as it is to see schools that are not prepared for emergency situations. I recently visited a Massachusetts middle school where I found almost every exterior door unlocked and hundreds of students in various parts of the school with no adult supervision. After nearly an hour wandering various parts of the school, I was finally asked by a teacher if I needed assistance. Though the school is in a relatively low crime area, thousands of criminal incidents occur due to poor school access control in other low crime communities, demonstrating how dangerous this situation is. A lack of any semblance of access control combined with almost non-existent student supervision is disturbing to say the least. Thankfully, most of the schools I visit are not this careless. While many schools could do a lot more, there has been considerable improvement in school safety and security in the past few decades with favorable results such as the noticeable drop in school homicides in American K–12 schools while the homicide rate has risen sharply in other countries such as England.

What can those who wish to help schools improve their security and safety do to help change the attitudes that have so often resulted in needless tragedy in schools? ...

Identifying Problems and Finding Solutions

Never in the history of our nation have educators been so pervasively focused on test scores. Driven by well-meaning government initiatives, the obsession with test scores has become so all encompassing that many educators push other critical issues like safety aside. This has caused many in the field of education to lose sight of the obvious—aids can't learn and teachers can't teach effectively in schools and classrooms that are not safe and orderly. Many of our clients feel that one of the most effective ways to improve test scores is to focus on safety.

About half of all school teachers leave the field of education within the first five years of service in the United States. Former teachers often report they decided to leave the field because of concerns relating to lack of safety, order and discipline. High turnover rates often affect support positions such as school bus drivers, school nurses and other support staff.

Many schools spend a lot on vandalism-related maintenance, theft, insurance premiums and litigation because of safety deficiencies. In major incidents, schools have lost millions. For example, one rural Oklahoma district spent one third of its annual budget in just 30 days following a single safety incident. A North Carolina district lost an entire high school due to an arson fire relating to poor access control, only to learn that there was a $15 million gap between the limits of their insurance coverage and the cost of rebuilding the school. More commonly, day-to-day costs can add up to significant expenditures. While many of these costs can be difficult to directly quantify, it is clear to us from our work with schools that schools can reduce fiscal waste by emphasizing safety.

School business officials are often concerned with the costs of litigation following safety incidents. It is not uncommon for schools with a high loss history to be strapped with very high insurance premiums for many years and for insurance companies to require significant future safety and security expenditures to maintain insurance coverage. A proactive approach to safety can reduce exposure to civil liability if an incident does take place.

Many school leaders fail to comprehend the tremendous loss of confidence that can accompany a series of school safety incidents or a single catastrophic event. Safety problems can be a "deal breaker" not only for the school or district, but for individual careers as well. One school system facing ongoing and significant safety issues closed nearly two dozen schools last year. In one multiple-victim school shooting case, seven educators ranging from the building principal to the school superintendent of schools left the district within one year of the shooting. For a school superintendent, "experienced a multiple-victim school shooting" is probably not a great enhancement to your resume.

Any school's first legal and moral obligation is the safety of students and staff. Safety is the right thing to do.

5

Foodservices Must Prepare for Disaster Recovery

Lisa White

Lisa White is a contributing editor to Foodservice Equipment & Supplies.

While most foodservice operations would not place disaster recovery planning at the top of their priority list, experts advise that efficient delivery of food supplies in a crisis is essential to the fast recovery of an affected area. Hospitals and schools in particular must plan for worst case scenarios and establish resources to ensure personnel receive food and water during a disaster.

Disaster plans are typically not at the top of most school and hospital foodservice operations' to-do list. Yet, many experts say they should be. Although the chances of a devastating hurricane, earthquake, terrorist attack or pandemic may be slim, the results can be catastrophic.

A survey by *KPMG Risk Advisory Services and Continuity Insights* magazine revealed that close to half of all businesses damaged in a disaster will close permanently. Despite the risk, only 32 percent of businesses have a disaster plan in place, according to a 2006 study by AMR Research, based in Boston.

"Foodservice is where the big hole is right now," says Gordon Meriwether, founder and principal of The Uriah Group, which assists companies in disaster planning and recovery.

Lisa White, "Planning Ahead," *Foodservice Equipment & Supplies*, vol. 60, no. 12, December 1, 2007, p. 24. Copyright © 2007 Reed Business Information, Inc. Reproduced by permission.

Meriwether has conducted a number of workshops for the foodservice industry on disaster planning, including 12 sessions for The National Society for Healthcare Foodservice Management (HFM). "Many people assume hospitals know what they are doing, but the focus in healthcare is on the surge of patients, not on the foodservice," he says.

In his workshops, Meriwether focuses on four principles of crisis management, which include leadership, communication, operations and finance. "The financial aspect of a crisis is always ignored, so I try to emphasize this. If there is no electrical power, businesses have no means to collect money or document their sales accurately. This deficit hits hard in the recovery phase following a disaster," he says.

In terms of leadership, Meriwether discusses succession planning and the need for, at minimum, a three-tier management structure. "This goes for a company's suppliers, as well. Everyone needs to know who they report to, the supplier tiers and their contact information," he says.

From an operations standpoint, it is critical to partner with county and city departments, including the local department of health.

The crisis communication plan needs to be well-thought-out and conveyed to all employees. "They need to know a plan is in place and what their role is," Meriwether says. It is also helpful to designate a communication professional familiar with crisis management to speak with the press in the event of a disaster.

From an operations standpoint, it is critical to partner with county and city departments, including the local department of health. "Knowing who wears what hat for the local government's public health, food and transportation is important," Meriwether says.

Hospital Handles Hurricane

A solid disaster plan gave East Jefferson General Hospital (EJGH) in Metairie, La., the distinction of being one of only three hospitals that remained open during Hurricane Katrina.

Michele Triche, the hospital's administrative director of food and nutrition, says this was due to EJGH's successful disaster plan, which was put into place two days before the hurricane hit. "The storm was predicted to hit Florida as opposed to New Orleans, so we didn't have a lot of time to prepare," she says.

Fortunately, EJGH had pre-approved contracts with all of its food and beverage vendors. "In the event of a hurricane, we have our orders pre-planned. We put the call in to our vendor and they deliver seven days worth of food. When Katrina was approaching, I placed the order on Saturday and the food, along with an air-conditioned truck to provide extra storage, was delivered the next day," Triche says.

The hospital's food and beverage supplier, located in Jackson, Miss., was unaffected by the storm.

Because EJGH was built in a flood zone, Triche decided to relocate the necessary foodservice equipment, including air curtain refrigerators, roaster ovens, a sandwich refrigerator, chafing dishes and food carts, to a third-floor location. The disaster plan designated employees who were responsible for moving each piece of equipment, and food was kept on pallets for easy transport.

The equipment was moved back into the first-floor kitchen after a day and a half, when it was determined that flooding would not be an issue.

Even though the hospital had no electricity for a couple of weeks and lost one generator, its remaining generators were sufficient. "We moved and consolidated patients and had rolling brownouts to help conserve our generator fuel," Triche says.

The hospital was fortunate to have its own water supply that was accessible during the storm. Natural gas service also was uninterrupted. In addition, written records were kept of all meals, since no one had access to money for payment.

Sanitation was another issue. Triche says liquid sanitizer, thermometers and a detailed temperature log were utilized and helped the hospital pass a health inspection following the storm.

EJGH's plan also included a detailed staffing list that separated employees into A, B and C lists, with A and B signifying essential personnel. "Katrina was such a monumental storm, however, that employees were evacuating the city, rather than reporting to work. I ended up operating with very minimal staff," Triche says.

Employees were responsible for bringing their own essentials, including bedding, flashlights, food, water and toiletries. After the storm had passed, the hospital worked with local and state agencies to bring employees back into the area.

Pandemic Planning

Bruce Thomas, associate vice president of guest services for Geisinger Health Systems in Danville, Pa., one of the largest rural healthcare systems in the nation, says his hospital takes a different approach to disaster planning. "Our focus has been on pandemic planning, rather than a natural or other disaster, though the plan is flexible," he says.

Before the plan was put in place, the company held organizational meetings for about a year, making sure each department had contingency plans in the event of an emergency. From a foodservice perspective, the main concern was the availability of food and beverages in storage.

"We identified how much product we have on hand at all times and then put contracts in place with our vendors outlining what we require in an emergency," Thomas says. "One of the things we stressed with our committee was the importance of foodservice staff to be notified as quickly as possible that this plan will be employed so we can begin storing food and purchasing in bulk from our vendors."

Like EJGH, Geisinger contracted with its food vendor to provide refrigerated trucks that run off of a gas compressor for additional storage. "Many people neglect to do this," Thomas says. Trailers provide a minimum of 800-square-feet of freezer space that can be sectioned off for refrigeration. The company also has prearranged contracts in emergency situations for bottled water from two separate sources. These contracts are updated annually.

Geisinger developed a menu to use during a pandemic. "It is broader and less diet-specific than our current menu, but we needed to define what would work for a specified period of time. We also recognized that we would see a higher percentage of patients and there will be more staff members that need to be fed during a pandemic," Thomas says.

Like hospitals, schools and universities need to understand the main functionality of the business, while catering to the foodservice operations that are vital during a disaster.

Because it is difficult to predict the size or effect of a pandemic, Geisinger considered the worst case scenario. "We needed to figure out how many meals we were serving daily and weekly, and then base our contingency plan on these numbers. Our patient potential is 11,000 meals a week or 1,500 meals per day," Thomas says.

Geisinger is looking into sourcing military-style meals or meals ready to eat (known as MREs), but Thomas says the high price tag may not be worth the insurance. "A four-week supply of MREs just for patient use would cost $500,000. There also is a shelf-life issue with these meals," Thomas says.

In terms of communication, Geisinger has maintained a list of home and cell phone numbers for its lead workers, including managers and supervisors, for the last three years. Also, two years ago the company implemented a program that has a foodservice manager on call 24/7. "We have a beeper that gets passed from manager to manager on a weekly basis. The person with the beeper is responsible for relating information to the team in the event of an emergency," Thomas says.

School Preparation

Like hospitals, schools and universities need to understand the main functionality of the business, while catering to the foodservice operations that are vital during a disaster.

Rafi Taherian, executive director of Stanford Dining at Stanford University in California, says because the foodservice program is not a stand-alone commercial operation, it needs to adhere to the university protocol.

Stanford's disaster plan focuses on three objectives, including protecting and preserving life; preserving university resources and assets; and resuming normal operation as quickly as possible. "We integrate these three rules into our foodservice plan," Taherian says.

Because disasters can have varying levels of intensity, the university had to consider that there may be work stoppage in one location or all locations. "Those are scenarios we have had to take into consideration," Taherian says. "At Stanford, we have planned for the worst case scenario."

Similar to Geisinger's plan, Stanford determined its maximum capacity and what it would need to have for the minimum level of preparation. "This information comes from the infrastructure we currently have and what the university expects us to do in the case of a disaster," Taherian says. The design of the current disaster plan allows the university to serve 17,000 people for five consecutive days.

According to the plan, the first step after a disaster is to assess the status of students and staff to account for everyone and ensure emergency safety and security protocols are in place. Second, staff assess damage to obtain data on the availability of resources and infrastructure. Subsequently, Stanford will focus on service methodology and food distribution. The university relies on advanced preparation meals, including dry foods and MREs. "We can't assume that we'll be able to produce hot meals," Taherian says.

"We have spreadsheets and formulas on how we will react with advanced prep food on hand," Taherian says. Four of the university's facilities feature emergency generating capacity to produce at least 72 hours worth of power. The remaining facilities are being retrofitted with these generators.

Taherian says Stanford's contingency plan is its emergency plan. "Looking at the many different scenarios that can occur in a disaster, we realize the plan is just a training document that provides us with ideas in an emergency so we are not put on the spot. It allows us to be prepared to make decisions and react without relying on a single individual," he says.

Learning from Experience

Louisiana State University put its emergency plan in place in 2005 during hurricanes Katrina and Rita, but soon realized where it was lacking. As a result, after the hurricanes the school instituted a three-deep backup policy recommended by the Federal Emergency Management Agency (FEMA).

Mark Kraner, director, contracted auxiliary services, says this plan is now reviewed and tweaked each year. "When hurricanes come into the Gulf of Mexico, our plan begins taking shape. Our first goal is to alert everyone on our staff who is essential to be prepared," he says.

LSU typically has at least two day's notice when a hurricane approaches, and makes its emergency decisions during this period. "We first determine which direction to take in terms of whether we need to order food. Since the eating habits of our clientele change dramatically during a hurricane, the food order changes." Kraner says.

Its plan calls for 2,000 essential personnel from campus to be on hand. "Prior to Katrina, we fed whoever showed up. This presented a problem tracking students. People utilized our food system and we had to take on the cost," Kraner says. "Our new procedure is to feed essential personnel first. We use a card system to document these food sales."

Before Katrina, the campus had never lost power for an extended period of time. Consequently, a backup generator provided power for freezers and coolers, but there was no gas for cooking and hoods weren't operable.

These difficulties during this catastrophic hurricane prompted LSU to rethink its disaster plan. "Now, we have a co-generation plan and are three-deep on everything we do," Kraner says. For example, along with the main electrical power from a local supplier, the school has a co-generation plant on campus as backup, along with large backup generators for its refrigeration and freezer units.

Because the generators cannot accommodate hood systems, LSU incorporated gas cooking equipment that can be converted to propane and used for cooking outside.

When its New Orleans food vendor was destroyed in the hurricane, the school realized it needed backup food and beverage suppliers that were out of the area. "Now, we have contracts for food orders from three separate warehouses outside of our area. Again, our backup is three-deep in this case," Kraner says.

Water was another issue during the hurricane that was not taken into account in the former plan. Luckily, when Katrina hit, the university was preparing for its first home football game. "We had 40 tons of ice and 100,000 bottles of beverages, mostly water, that we were able to tap into. But we were lucky," Kraner says.

Now, the plan is to start bringing water to the campus on July 1 each year, with the goal of accumulating 100,000 bottled beverages by Aug. 1 or the start of hurricane season. "We also have an agreement with a local soft-drink provider to bring beverages in on an as-needed basis as well as a similar arrangement with another beverage supplier. In addition, we have a campus well we can tap into. This is in line with our three-deep plan," Kraner says.

Space has been designated in residence halls that include bedding, showers and toiletry kits for emergency personnel. "We also have a two-day supply of MREs for emergency personnel. So if I lose everything in the dining hall and concessions areas, we still have MREs in cold storage. I also have a standing agreement with our MRE vendor to provide more meals within 48 hours of a disaster," Kraner says.

Although it is difficult to prepare for the unknown, the importance of having a disaster plan in place cannot be overstated.

Coordinating Communication

Unlike before Katrina, LSU now has a centralized communication center. "During Katrina and Rita, I operated the foodservice separate from the campus. Now, during an emergency, I work directly with campus training personnel, and staff members are aware of our capabilities and resources," Kraner says. He keeps a central list of resources, along with the name and number of suppliers, accessible to other team members so no one is reliant on him to set up and put a plan in operation. "I have a couple layers of people to work with and the campus has a ton of resources, phone systems, computers systems and space to put a plan into action quickly."

There also is one point of communication to make sure resources are allocated properly. LSU works closely with the state and is tied into emergency groups to enhance communication during a disaster.

"We are now better prepared. Everyone knows what their job is if and when there is an emergency. New hires are told if they are essential personnel and, if so, what the expectations are in a disaster," Kraner says.

Although it is difficult to prepare for the unknown, the importance of having a disaster plan in place cannot be overstated. "Foodservice operations need to put together an organized agenda and try to think of as many things as they can in terms of coping with a disaster to be as prepared as possible," Thomas says. It is a matter of survival.

6

Courts Should Make Disaster Recovery Planning a Priority

Dan Heilman

Dan Heilman is a staff writer for Minnesota Lawyer.

Across the country, state and local governments are learning from recent events including 9/11, Hurricane Katrina and the southern California fires how to better prepare their citizens for an emergency. Minnesota courts are undertaking an ambitious effort to implement an effective statewide disaster contingency plan.

In a post-9/11, post-Katrina world, disaster contingency has become a more and more prominent issue for all kinds of businesses as they struggle with the issue of how they would bounce back in the face of a catastrophe.

Minnesota's courts are no different, and the state's court system as a whole is undertaking an ambitious effort to make itself as prepared as possible in the event of a disaster.

The courts have been spending about a year gearing up for the implementation of a disaster contingency plan that would lay out specific procedures in the wake of any event that might disrupt the court's work. That could mean anything from a terrorist threat to a gas leak to a natural disaster, such as the flooding that struck southeastern Minnesota earlier this year.

Clerk of Appellate Courts Fred Grittner, the lead coordinator on the project, said the purpose of the plan is to prepare any of Minnesota's 87 trial courts to react quickly if they had to adapt to a disaster. The plan is slated to enter pilot project phase early next year.

"If there's a flood like the one in southeastern Minnesota, and the courthouse has to be abandoned, what can you do within the first 48 hours to make sure you can set up shop and keep going?" he asked rhetorically. "Do you have someplace where you can move the courthouse's functions? The idea is to name the potential risks, then do an impact analysis and figure out how we would respond."

Learning from Experience

The need for a disaster contingency plan specific to America's courts gained momentum after Hurricane Katrina in 2005, when several courthouses in and around New Orleans ended up under water, and court employees had to scramble to complete the most basic court functions.

In the wake of that disaster, the National Conference of Chief Justices and State Court Administrators have passed resolutions supporting a number of initiatives related to disaster recovery, and the National Center for State Courts has set up a website with resources for court systems that are developing their own plans.

Chief Justice Russell Anderson pushed strongly for Minnesota to develop a contingency plan, and with the support of State Court Administrator Sue Dosal, the state Judicial Council endorsed its development [in early 2007].

Corporations can figure out how much money they'd lose every day they're not open . . . But for the courts, it's things like how many filing fees aren't going to be collected, or parking tickets paid.

The need for a plan in Minnesota was reinforced for Grittner during a National Center for State Courts seminar last

July [2007]. At the seminar, a county court administrator from Ohio said a disgruntled litigant had poured 1½ pounds of mercury into several areas of the courthouse.

"That's not the kind of thing you expect to happen, but it happened, and it took more than a week to decontaminate the courthouse," said Grittner.

Sending Cases to the Front of the Line

Grittner's office has been using the past year to pick the brains of workers from courts throughout Minnesota and throughout the United States—not only to find out what has and hasn't worked in other locales, but to assemble as many "what if?" scenarios as possible.

For instance, say the court's computer network goes down. Files are backed up, but if there was a major virus that somehow disabled the court's case management system, the courts would need a means to mimic how they do their docket entries so that data can easily be re-keyed into the court's database once the network is back up.

Even if a disaster didn't incapacitate the physical court building, there can be human-resources issues to consider.

"Corporations can figure out how much money they'd lose every day they're not open," Grittner said. "But for the courts, it's things like how many filing fees aren't going to be collected, or parking tickets paid. All of a sudden, a number of income streams drop."

Then there are practical matters to consider if a courthouse is put out of commission. Courts are being asked to scout nearby locations where they could temporarily set up shop, as well as assembling a list of crucial equipment and supplies they would need in order to resume work.

Each court will have separate teams that will see to operational oversight (addressing issues of command structure), logistics (where the court will move if necessary, which supplies are needed), technology and general recovery.

Even if a disaster didn't incapacitate the physical court building, there can be human-resources issues to consider. Grittner said a number of court employees near the areas hit by floods [in 2007] had to miss work because they were bailing water from their own houses or helping elderly relatives.

Another issue the courts must keep in mind is how they would perform "triage" with cases in the event of a disaster. At the trial court level, cases involving criminal law would get priority, along with things like emergency orders and mandated hearings, because of the constitutional rights of the accused to face arraignment within a prescribed amount of time.

"Those would take precedence over parking tickets and civil awsuits," said Grittner.

Using Technology to Prepare for Future Disasters

A Minneapolis software developer is helping the courts face the task of getting everyone on the same page of preparedness. The courts are using a customized version of LBL Technologies' ContingencyPro program during all phases of the effort, including follow-up and maintenance.

LBL managing director Geoff Wold said the program helps facilitate development of a disaster contingency plan with the use of dozens of fill-in-the-blank templates that are specific to Minnesota's court system, as well as regularly prompting users to update the database with personnel moves, phone number updates and other changes.

"The last thing you want is to get all that information into the program only to have it sit on a shelf for two years and become outdated by the time you need it," said Wold.

The program also automatically publishes the latest-updated plan to an offsite Internet address, so that it's always accessible if disaster strikes the site of the court's main server.

Working with a development budget of $100,000, the contingency project's pilot stage—in which each individual court will identify its own priorities, potential risk areas and other contingency factors—is set to be completed in March.

From there, coordinators in each court will learn the ContingencyPro software and spend the summer completing their individual contingency plans in anticipation of wrapping up the creation phase of the project by this time next year.

But maintenance of the disaster contingency plan will have to be carefully monitored and maintained as different scenarios become evident, said Grittner.

"It's just the beginning of a process that will become part of the judicial business culture," he said. "It really makes you think about your work: Who are our customers, who are the people who serve us, and who do we call if they're not there?"

7

Healthcare Systems Should Prepare to Track Patients During Disasters

Robin Blair

Robin Blair is the editor of Health Management Technology.

Hurricane Katrina revealed several weaknesses in disaster recovery planning at local, state, and federal levels. Perhaps the most significant of these weaknesses was the inability to monitor patients effectively during evacuation and treatment. Now, healthcare providers are working to develop a system for tracking patients that can always be accessed in a disaster.

Is there anyone who doesn't remember Hurricane Katrina and the heart-wrenching TV images of traumatized New Orleans residents being herded onto buses and then disbursed and displaced into Utah, Texas, Arkansas and Georgia? More than any political speech or legislative initiative, Hurricane Katrina drove home the hardest of healthcare lessons: The time to prepare for disaster is before it strikes.

In New England, a small but mighty collaboration of medical, IT and volunteer personnel has heeded the warning. New Hampshire-based Dartmouth-Hitchcock Medical Center, IT supplier athenahealth Inc. of Watertown, Mass. and dozens of New Hampshire volunteers, with support from the Department of Homeland Security's Northern New England Metro-

Robin Blair, "Disaster-Proof Patients: Healthcare Providers and IT Supplier in New England Simulate a Disaster Situation to Test a Web-Based EMR for Regional and Maybe National Adoption," *Health Management Technology*, vol. 28, no. 2, February 2007, pp. 44–46. Copyright © 2007 Nelson Publishing. Reproduced by permission.

politan Medical Response System (NNE MMRS), staged a 1-day medical emergency simulation on Nov. 15, 2006, to test an emergency response model using the Web-based athenaNet platform.

The objective was simple: Simulate a disaster and test the creation of a Web-based electronic medical record (EMR) that could service all affected patients regardless of location. The planning and execution, however, weren't simple. They required elbow grease.

Track, Treat and Record Patients Effectively

During any mass casualty episode, be it a terrorist attack, pandemic event or a natural disaster, "We have an enormous problem keeping track of what we do to and with patients," says Dartmouth-Hitchcock Medical Center's Medical Director for Emergency Response, Robert Gougelet, M.D., who also serves as program director for the NNE MMRS. He says that during events such as Hurricane Katrina or the SARS emergency, "We need to keep track of patients, of how we treat them, when and where we treat them, what medications they receive, what procedures are done, which facilities they visit and for how long they remain under our care. Those are the basics we should be doing. In the past, we have seriously struggled with these because we have been forced to do them manually," and with no continuity of record keeping.

The NNE MMRS/athenahealth pilot, if expanded, would erase the manual portion of that equation and would offer extensive potential for continuity of data.

The NNE MMRS/athenahealth team utilized 50 high school student volunteers acting as patients impacted by an emergency, who were then "treated" in area facilities for a wide range of medical conditions. The demonstration utilized athenaNet, a Web-based platform that functions as the backbone of athenahealth's practice management system, supplying the foundation for billing rules, electronic eligibility checking, scheduling, claims submission and reporting. The system runs with as little as a PC, a browser and an Internet connection. During the simulation, healthcare providers were able to create individual EMRs for every patient seen via athenaClinicals, a Web-based EMR service hosted on athenaNet.

"The objective," says Gougelet "was to track each patient from the point that he or she entered the healthcare system during an emergency and then be able to create and build a usable EMR for that patient, regardless of entry point. We know that during emergencies, patients don't come equipped with their medical records. At best, some may have two or three photocopied documents about medications or medical histories. Even if hospitals do use EMRs or electronic charting, they may be unable to access their data during an emergency, and they certainly can't exchange data with other providers in a disaster-struck region. With the athenahealth EMR, we were able to create a record for each patient. A record that every provider involved in treating that patient could access and augment."

Gougelet says this is critical in a crisis. Many patients will have one healthcare encounter, and they're done. But in most emergency situations, some patients will experience two or three episodes of treatment by different providers at different types of facilities, possibly in different locales, or over a prolonged period of time. The demonstration proved that patients could be transported and moved among facilities in different locations without detrimental impact on any provider's ability to access patient data or to add to it.

Assessing the Big Picture

Pilots and demos are one thing. Real metropolitan or regional emergencies are another. But Gougelet and his teams, both at Dartmouth-Hitchcock and at the NNE MMRS, are experts. They talk routinely in terms of disaster-site triage, triage tags, resource mobilization, medical strike teams, surge capacity and "distributing" patients to alternate care facilities, terms well outside the norm of typical healthcare lingo.

Theirs is an unusual challenge in terms of preparing for disaster. NNE MMRS is the first Metropolitan Medical Response System in the nation to develop a multistate project. Together, Maine, Vermont and New Hampshire constitute a condensed geographical area, largely rural in nature, and yet one that includes an international border, an Atlantic seacoast and multiple, potential urban targets to the south in Boston, Hartford and even New York City. It is a perfect place to launch an emergency simulation.

"We have a system here that could be developed and adopted as a national system," says Gougelet. "We anticipated this before the pilot and are convinced of it now. The system creates a unique EMR with a unique numerical identifier for each patient. We can create such a record from triage tags from the field, even if we lack the patient's name. If the tag has a bar code and location, we can bring data into the athenahealth system where the EMR starts and then can create a data collection that can be accessed by any provider treating the patient, even in another community or another state. All along the way, data can be added to the patient's record. We can even follow patients for 15 or 20 years with these records. This is what lends accountability to providing healthcare. True accountability of this nature doesn't exist today."

Hospitals and communities can't support all this emergency medical care on their own. There should be a mechanism open for data collection and billing, in the event that the care is reimbursable.

Nevertheless, Gougelet stipulates that such success is the tip of the iceberg and that much work remains. Interfacing with field tracking and resource sharing software, such as HC Standard, and the development of templates and front-end pages are primary examples. He estimates that up to 25 different kinds of emergency situations exist for which dozens of templates can and should be built, so that communities are ready for almost any crisis. "Anthrax, for example," he says. "We know the symptoms and treatments. We can build templates into the system for Anthrax-related disaster, combine them with user-friendly, pull-down menus and then tie the software back to an interface that is friendly and fast. Templates like this also can be designed on the fly, because the system is centralized."

Managing Reimbursement

In a true emergency, providers probably don't think much about coding, claims and reimbursement. "When we started the project," says Gougelet, "reimbursement was of absolutely no concern to me. That wasn't how I thought about disasters. But as we moved further into planning and held briefings, the issue became clearer. Hospitals and communities can't support all this emergency medical care on their own. There should be a mechanism open for data collection and billing, in the event that the care is reimbursable."

We can prevent the confusion that was experienced so vividly by patients and medical personnel during Hurricane Katrina.

Indeed, there is a mechanism. The athenahealth system tracks and records everything in the background; that includes the provider, the facility, patient by numerical identifier or name, symptoms, diagnosis, treatment rendered, medications distributed, procedures performed and subsequent referral. According to athenahealth Director of Revenue Cycle Product Management Bob Gatewood, the system operates like this behind the scenes because "Dr. Gougelet is right. Physicians, triage nurses and EMTs don't want to think about having to collect and store data in the midst of an emergency, when hundreds or even thousands of people need help."

The most that can be expected of medical personnel in a real crisis, he says, is that they can electronically document how and when they encounter and treat each patient. "So, we designed the system to keep track of everything for them, but in the background. If there is reimbursement out there that can compensate for emergency medical services, this system will apply codes to the captured data so reimbursement can be sought as soon as it is feasible."

As the athenahealth system evolves toward servicing communities and regions in crisis situations, it works in ways geared to best support emergency medical needs. According to Gatewood, "We can put huge volumes of data into the system in advance. We can load in facility, trauma center and treatment capability information, plus data about all providers in a region—physicians, nurses, EMTs—and their locations and skill levels. Literally, we can create a database for a community. Then, if an emergency strikes, we can show up with a laptop and make use of all the data via an Internet connection. We can prevent the confusion that was experienced so vividly by patients and medical personnel during Hurricane Katrina."

Forecast for the Future

The system provides another advantage that both providers and first responders will appreciate. The continual data capture can be used for more than creating claims and seeking reimbursement; it also can be used for modeling and forecasting. While some people think the spitting out of reports is boring—and sometimes it is—the spitting out of reports that can extrapolate and predict for community leaders and first responders what they can expect in pandemic or emergency situations can prove invaluable.

How fast will a disease spread in a given population and where will it spread first? What ratio of patients coming to a hospital will need only minimal services, compared to those who will need maximum-level services? Which patients will arrive first? How fast will a current supply of medications be consumed? A community or region that could answer those questions in advance would be light years ahead of others in terms of disaster preparedness.

The very term "disaster preparedness" means preparing in advance for the future, and that's a concept Gougelet et al. currently embrace. The next step, he says, after data from the November emergency exercise is shared with and analyzed by surrounding states, is to identify funding sources and pursue future funding for project expansion. "In New Hampshire alone, we have 26 hospitals. We can query each: What kind of EMR do you have? What would you do if you lost patient records? We can begin to customize how we use the athenahealth system so that it meets a variety of medical needs throughout New Hampshire, and then Vermont and Maine as well."

While Gougelet talks confidently of identifying funding sources, seeking funding, expanding the pilot, analyzing more data, looking at reports, gathering and considering opinions, in the end, he remains a man of few words. He feels strongly, however, that this is a critical step forward in our national preparedness efforts.

8

Insurers Need to Have Disaster Recovery Plans

Nathan Conz

Nathan Conz is the associate editor of Insurance & Technology.

When disaster strikes, those affected need to contact their insurance company immediately. If insurers do not have a plan for relocation and access to resources when their primary offices are closed and employees are displaced, clients cannot get the help they need. There are several steps insurance companies should take to ensure smooth operations even in times of severe crisis.

In October [2007], more than 20 wildfires blazed a path of destruction through seven Southern California counties. According to Boston-based catastrophe risk modeler AIR Worldwide, more than 1,800 homes had been destroyed and 490,000 acres of land had been consumed by Oct. 26. AIR estimates the insured losses from the wildfires will total at least $1.5 billion.

Largely unnoticed among those staggering statistics, however, were the 36 commercial properties that were lost to the fires and the untold number of businesses that were affected by the catastrophe. Depending on an organization's disaster preparedness, those losses and disruptions could have crippled critical business processes, toppling customer service levels and bottom lines alike.

Nathan Conz, "Preparing for the Worst: To Maintain Operations and Service Levels in the Face of a Catastrophe, Insurers Increasingly Are Viewing Disaster Recovery Plans as Full-Fledged Business Initiatives That Must Be Constantly Updated to Account for New Developments," *Insurance & Technology*, vol. 33, no. 1, January 2008, pp. 30–34. Reproduced by permission.

For insurers, especially those that do a sizable amount of business in their own backyards, business continuity planning (BCP) has emerged as a key imperative. During times of catastrophe, an insurance organization can find itself in a precarious position—large numbers of customers are likely to demand immediate service at a time when the business processes that support that service could be most vulnerable.

As a result, disaster recovery—specifically as it pertains to data backup and recovery—must be measured in minutes, as opposed to days or even weeks. Therefore, questions regarding data preservation and recovery, and resource planning and deployment, are at the forefront of insurance executives' minds. But it hasn't always been that way.

According to Michael Costonis, the Philadelphia-based executive director of Accenture's global claims practice, the depth of insurers' BCP has changed as a result of recent catastrophes, starting with the Sept. 11 terrorist attacks and continuing with several recent natural disasters. "[Business continuity questions] have become, in a lot of instances, the gatekeeper questions as opposed to the clean-up questions because the issue has become that important," he says.

In fact, many insurers are approaching the issue as less of an isolated IT challenge and more as a business challenge. At Pacific Life, for example, the strategic shift began in 2003, says Carl B. Jackson, BCP director for the Newport Beach, Calif.-based carrier. "Our business continuity planning philosophy was basically IT-centric, as it was at many organizations," he recalls.

"Through regulatory emphasis; through audit; through leading practices; and through customer, vendor and business partner contacts; it has become evident to us that just planning to recover our IT infrastructure is not enough," Jackson continues. "We really need to focus not just on IT. As a matter of fact, [we shouldn't focus] on IT at all in the beginning, but on business processes and understanding the time-critical nature of those business processes."

Sometimes the threat of catastrophe—and accompanying precautionary evacuations—can be just as disruptive from a workforce perspective.

Much in the same way that chief technology officers are evolving into more well-rounded chief information officers, disaster recovery plans are beginning to evolve as well—from "set it and forget it" IT protocols and procedures buried in static three-ring binders to full-fledged business initiatives that are constantly updated to account for new developments and risks. "The old-style method of business continuity planning was very much inward-focused. It was very much operations-focused," Accenture's Costonis adds. "Now the new method that is being demanded of insurance companies involves understanding current and potential macro risks and what it really means to respond to those."

Too Close for Comfort

If the recent business continuity experiences of some insurance organizations are any indication, a catastrophe doesn't have to physically touch a company's building to rock the status quo. Sometimes the threat of catastrophe—and accompanying precautionary evacuation—can be just as disruptive from a workforce perspective.

Pacific Life (more than $100 billion in assets) was one of many companies affected by the recent California wildfires. While the insurer's Newport Beach headquarters was not threatened by the flames, its Foothill Ranch, Calif., facility—comprised of two buildings housing 540 employees and a substantial call center operation—is located just a few blocks from the hills where a fire raged during the fourth week of October [2007].

"It wasn't so much the fire that threatened our facility as it was the heavy smoke," explains [Carl B.] Jackson. "People were having trouble breathing."

Jackson says he was first notified that the Foothill Ranch location might need to be evacuated on Sunday night, Oct. 21; by Monday morning, it was apparent that the smoke would pose a real problem. Further, many area schools were evacuated, forcing workers with children to plan accordingly.

"Our business processes were not in danger at any time," Jackson says when describing the situation on Monday, Oct. 22. "It was strictly people availability that was an issue."

As workers shuffled in and out of the Foothill Ranch buildings on Monday, Jackson established and set up an incident command center (ICC) at Pacific Life's Newport Beach headquarters. "We monitored the situation throughout the day," he relates. But, "We didn't activate any business continuity plans or declare any sort of disaster."

If service levels suffer due to poor disaster recovery planning, satisfaction levels, and possibly retention rates, can drop accordingly.

But while Pacific Life was able to go about business as usual that Monday, Port Arthur, Texas-based Talon Insurance Agency was not so lucky in 2003 when the threat of Hurricane Lily forced an evacuation of its headquarters. Having just formed after the merger of two local agencies in May 2001, Talon had spent most of its energy pulling the business together and had not yet formed any meaningful business continuity plans, according to Talon operations manager Linda Trevino.

As an independent agency, Talon shares many of the same business continuity challenges as a carrier. Often, clients look to their agents as the first point of contact when reporting a claim. If service levels suffer due to poor disaster recovery planning, satisfaction levels, and possibly retention rates, can drop accordingly.

Preparation or Panic

When it was clear authorities would order an evacuation, Trevino says, she and another employee drove to the agency's headquarters at 5 A.M. and had only 45 minutes to remove critical hardware, equipment and data. "During that time, it became very evident that we did not have a plan," she admits. Servers were dismantled and placed in vehicles for evacuation, Trevino recalls. In doing so, the company's Houston office also was brought offline, and phone calls to the Port Arthur location were unable to be forwarded.

As it turns out, Hurricane Lily missed the region. Still, the mere threat of catastrophe caused Talon's business to go down for three days. "That's loss of productivity; that's lack of service to our clients," Trevino says. "It was very unacceptable. We knew we had to do something to keep that from ever happening again."

While the mere threat of disaster can disrupt an insurer's business, the ramifications multiply when a catastrophe makes good on its threat.

By Wednesday, Oct. 24, the smoke that loomed near Pacific Life's Foothill Ranch facility the previous two days had inched closer. With the fire on the move and smoke issues worsening, management made the decision to activate a strategy that had been developed by a business continuity team in the days before—to move about 50 people, primarily call center agents and support staff, to the Newport Beach office. "In case the [Foothill Ranch] building needed to be evacuated, there would be no interruption in service," Jackson explains.

Preparation for that move actually had started on Monday, with IT workers transforming the Newport Beach location's conference center into a temporary, but fully equipped, call center, according to Jackson. Displaced workers began arriving on Wednesday morning, and all 50 people had been accommodated by noon.

Jackson says that the maneuvering was almost entirely seamless from the customer point of view. "We were able to accommodate all [our call center workers'] needs," he asserts. "When they plugged into our network here at Newport Beach, they had all the facilities they needed."

Divide and Conquer

A key to the success of Pacific Life's plan, and to many other business continuity efforts, was the decision to divide the increased workload among the insurer's other locations. Jackson says that the carrier leveraged its interactive voice response (IVR) platform and automated voice recognition system to route incoming calls. Calls from producers were handled by the temporary call center set up in Newport Beach. Incoming policyholder calls, meanwhile, were directed to the company's tertiary facility in Omaha.

"We split the load from a customer service standpoint, and [the two facilities] were able to satisfactorily cover both sides," Jackson says. A day later the fire had moved south, and by the afternoon of Friday, Oct. 26, the business continuity plan was deactivated.

If the location had ever been truly compromised, or if the carrier's headquarters should ever find itself paralyzed from disaster, Pacific Life has the ability to move its processing capabilities to its Omaha location, Jackson notes. To support any such move, he says, the carrier has analyzed its processes and specifically prioritized a set of what it calls Tier 1 business processes that help determine which functions are most time-critical in the event of a business disruption.

"About one-third to one-half of what any company does is time-critical, so it's important—if we want to drive down the cost and expense impact of doing business continuity planning—to focus our efforts only on those business processes that are the most time-critical," Jackson says.

Leveraging satellite offices and locations also has helped the Talon Insurance Agency handle increased workloads in the face of disaster, particularly in 2004, when a fire started by a faulty power strip severely damaged its main office, requiring extensive renovations. "Looking from the outside of the building, you could barely tell that there had been a fire, but the inside was totally devastated," relates the company's Trevino. "There was nothing unaffected. We still have files that smell like smoke."

However, in the months immediately preceding the fire, Talon had finalized a deal with AMS Services (Bothell, Wash.), its agency management system vendor, for a disaster recovery service. The agency also had worked with its local phone carrier to set up an automatic call-forwarding service to Talon's satellite offices.

With the revamped business continuity plan in place, Talon was able to immediately route calls to its Houston and Tyler, Texas, offices. The results were apparent almost immediately, according to Trevino. By 5 P.M. on the day of the fire the agency had sent its backup tapes to AMS, and by the next day, AMS was able to provide Talon workers with remote, online access to its agency management system. "AMS was able to just take our data and put it into their environment to make it [available] online so we could access it from any of our locations," Trevino says.

While the company endured two days of disruptions, almost none was apparent to clients, Trevino insists. Despite the magnitude of the fire and the in-house location of Talon's agency management system servers, less than one day of data was lost, she adds.

Web-Based Advantages

Having realized the benefits of a Web-based system during its disaster recovery effort, the Talon Insurance Agency quickly made a decision to migrate from its legacy AMS AfW agency management system, which ran on servers located inside its offices, to AMS'; Web-based AfW Online. "We recognized that, because of our location on the Gulf Coast near the Texas-Louisiana border, that was the key to our disaster recovery plan [as it pertained] to providing services to our clients," Trevino explains.

Once again, a revamped Talon business continuity plan was soon put to the test. This time, it was September 2005's Hurricane Rita that forced an evacuation of the region. With its incoming calls already routed to its other offices and its data now hosted off-site, Talon's employees were able to focus on the evacuation effort, which was especially comforting, Trevino notes, given that Hurricane Katrina had ravaged parts of nearby Louisiana just a month before.

Focus on key issues, which often end up being very simple, such as ensuring that everyone is equipped with an up-to-date phone tree to facilitate communication.

This time, Talon's down time lasted only a handful of minutes. The agency's Tyler location handled incoming claims, while the Houston office supported ongoing business. Some of the agency's competitors, meanwhile, were only able to tack 1-800 numbers on the doors to their shuttered offices. And even then, power outages shut down some of those phone lines, according to Trevino.

"We didn't get back into our home office—we could not because we didn't have power—for three weeks but functioned perfectly," Trevino recalls. As a result, Talon earned a quick but long-lasting customer service win with customers, who saw their claims handled in a timely fashion while their neighbors struggled to reach other agencies.

"If we hadn't been baptized by fire and by Hurricane Lily, we may not have placed the same emphasis [on disaster recovery]," Trevino relates. "It's a real disadvantage to take the attitude that it won't happen to you. It can happen, and it can happen extremely quickly."

The Simple Things

Drawing on more disaster recovery experience in the past five years than most carriers or producers will see in a lifetime, Trevino warns others in the industry to avoid focusing too much on developing exhaustive business continuity procedures and documents. "if you're in the middle of a disaster, you aren't going to go look for a [BCP] book—and if you are, there's something wrong with you," Trevino says. "That's not the proper response to a disaster."

Instead, Trevino suggests, focus on key issues, which often end up being very simple, such as ensuring that everyone is equipped with an up-to-date phone tree to facilitate communication.

To keep the lines of communication open, Pacific Life leverages Wayne, Pa.-based SunGard's Paragon software to allow for online access to business continuity plans for roughly 50 different business divisions. The system includes an automated notification capability called MIR3, which Pacific Life's Jackson identifies as a key component to disaster recovery. "It allows us—through templates, call trees or team lists—to almost instantaneously notify large numbers of people with a specific message," he explains.

Like Trevino, Jackson says he does not focus too much of his energy on developing static documents, such as manuals and IT protocols. Rather, he suggests, promoting a culture of business continuity awareness may be the most important action taken by an insurer when preparing for an eventual disaster.

"BCP is really not a technological issue—it's a people issue. If the people don't know how we're going to recover, they're not going to recover," Jackson explains. "Frequent testing and awareness in this area with the people is far more important than spending an inordinate amount of time documenting recovery procedures."

9

Feuds Between State and Federal Governments Slow Recovery Efforts

Aaron C. Davis

Aaron C. Davis is a member of the Associated Press.

During the southern California wildfires of 2007, fingerpointing between state and federal officials occurred when two dozen water-dropping helicopters remained grounded due to miscommunication and a lack of trained personnel. This feud wasted valuable time and resources that might otherwise have saved some of the half-million acres that were destroyed by the flames.

State and federal officials . . . blamed each other for allowing nearly two dozen water-dropping helicopters to sit idle while deadly wildfires ravaged Southern California, and Gov. Arnold Schwarzenegger pledged to improve the state's response to battling wildfires [in October 2007].

The head of the state's firefighting agency lashed out at the Marines and U.S. Forest Service, saying the military had failed to commit to the training necessary to launch helicopters more quickly. The Forest Service had neglected to provide enough helicopter managers to launch the aircrafts when they became available, he said.

"We're getting all of this criticism and I don't want to get into saying it should have been the Forest Service, should have been the Marines," said Ruben Grijalva, chief of the California

Aaron C. Davis, "Fingerpointing Ensues over Copters Grounded During California Wildfires," *USA Today*, October 27, 2007. www.usatoday.com. Reproduced by permission of the author.

Department of Forestry and Fire Protection. "But that's why I'm talking today because it's affecting the morale of this organization."

The Forest Service disputed Grijalva's claim, saying that providing fire spotters for Marines wasn't solely a federal responsibility. Forest Service officials also cast doubt on assertions by members of the military and several members of California's Congressional delegation that the Marine helicopters were ready days before they were called into action.

Dennis Hulbert, Regional Aviation Officer for the U.S. Forest Service in California, said the Marines were primarily responsible for the delay.

"They had their own problems," he said.

In a time of crisis, the rules did not serve our country well . . . the bureaucrats lost picture of what their mission is, to protect the citizens.

According to Hulbert, it took the Marines a day to outfit their helicopters with buckets to fight the fires. Once they did, they directed those resources first to fight fires on military land. It wasn't until [later] that they were used to fight fires elsewhere in Southern California, he said. . . .

"We are overwhelmed with bureaucratic regulations and the spotters are the best example of that," said U.S. Rep. Dana Rohrabacher. "In a time of crisis, the rules did not serve our country well . . . the bureaucrats lost picture of what their mission is, to protect the citizens."

Fingerpointing Wastes Precious Time

The fingerpointing ensued after The Associated Press reported . . . that nearly two dozen military helicopters, including those from the Marines, Navy and California National Guard, stayed grounded for at least a day after several wildfires broke out because of bureaucracy, including rules that so-called "fire spotters" must be on board each helicopter. Spotters were not available for all the aircraft ready to fight the fire. Fire officials ultimately abandoned the rule, but only after more than 1,000 homes had been destroyed.

The AP also reported that two of the California National Guard's C-130 cargo planes couldn't help because they've yet to be outfitted with tanks needed to carry thousands of gallons of fire retardant, though that was promised four years ago.

The fingerpointing did little to clarify whether fire officials effectively marshaled all available aerial resources to put out the flames before they grew into a conflagration that charred a half-million acres and destroyed over 1,700 homes.

Instead, the remarks seemed to reinforce that a complicated bureaucracy and set of rules governing the use of military aircraft to fight fires had stalled the response.

Gov. Arnold Schwarzenegger acknowledged . . . that it appeared the firefighting effort could have been more effective if enough so-called "fire spotters," also called helicopter managers, had been available to launch the aircraft. . . .

"There are things that we could improve on and I think this is what we are going to do because a disaster like this, you know, really, in the end is a good vehicle, a motivator for everyone to come together," said Schwarzenegger in response to questions about grounded aircraft. "I remember after Katrina, as sad as it is, but it takes sometimes a disaster like this to really wake everyone up and affect things."

10

Government Failure to Heed Disaster Warnings Costs Lives

Spencer S. Hsu

Spencer S. Hsu is a staff writer for the Washington Post.

House investigators determined that the loss of life sustained during Hurricane Katrina might have been avoided if government officials, particularly Homeland Security, heeded warnings issued by disaster planners in 2004. A lack of preparation and delay in response led to unnecessary deaths.

Hurricane Katrina exposed the U.S. government's failure to learn the lessons of the Sept. 11, 2001, terrorist attacks, as leaders from President Bush down disregarded ample warnings of the threat to New Orleans and did not execute emergency plans or share information that would have saved lives, according to a blistering report by House investigators.

A draft of the report, to be released publicly Wednesday, includes 90 findings of failures at all levels of government, according to a senior investigation staffer who requested anonymity because the document is not final. Titled "A Failure of Initiative," it is one of three separate reviews by the House, Senate and White House that will in coming weeks dissect the response to the nation's costliest natural disaster.

The 600-plus-page report lays primary fault with the passive reaction and misjudgments of top Bush aides, singling out Homeland Security Secretary Michael Chertoff, the Homeland Security Operations Center and the White House Home-land Security Council, according to a 60-page summary of the document obtained by *The Washington Post*. Regarding Bush, the report found that "earlier presidential involvement could have speeded the response" because he alone could have cut through all bureaucratic resistance.

The report, produced by an 11-member House select com-mittee of Republicans chaired by Rep. Thomas M. Davis III, proposes few specific changes. But it is an unusual compen-dium of criticism by the House GOP, which generally has not been aggressive in its oversight of the administration.

The Cost of Delayed Response

The report portrays Chertoff, who took the helm of the de-partment six months before the storm, as detached from events. It contends he switched on the government's emer-gency response systems "late, ineffectively or not at all," delay-ing the flow of federal troops and materiel by as much as three days.

The White House did not fully engage the president or "substantiate, analyze and act on the information at its dis-posal," failing to confirm the collapse of New Orleans's levee system on Aug. 29 [2005] the day of Katrina's landfall, which led to catastrophic flooding of the city of 500,000 people.

Weaknesses identified by Sept. 11 investigators—poor communications among first responders, a shortage of qualified emergency personnel and lack of training and funding—doomed a response confronted by overwhelm-ing demands for help.

On the ground, Federal Emergency Management Agency director Michael D. Brown, who has since resigned, FEMA field commanders and the U.S. military's commanding general set up rival chains of command. The Coast Guard, which alone rescued nearly half of 75,000 people stranded in New Orleans, flew nine helicopters and two airplanes over the city that first day, but eyewitness reconnaissance did not reach official Washington before midnight.

At the same time, weaknesses identified by Sept. 11 investigators—poor communications among first responders, a shortage of qualified emergency personnel and lack of training and funding—doomed a response confronted by overwhelming demands for help.

"If 9/11 was a failure of imagination then Katrina was a failure of initiative. It was a failure of leadership," the report's preface states. "In this instance, blinding lack of situational awareness and disjointed decision making needlessly compounded and prolonged Katrina's horror."

Chertoff spokesman Russ Knocke said, "every ounce of authority" and "100 percent of everything that could be pre-staged was pre-staged" by the federal government before landfall once the president signed emergency disaster declarations on Aug. 27 [2005] Brown had "all authority" to make decisions and requests, and his "willful insubordination . . . was a significant problem" for Chertoff, Knocke said.

White House spokesman Trent Duffy said Bush had full confidence in his homeland security team, both appointed and career. "The president was involved from beginning to end," implementing emergency powers before the storm and taking responsibility afterward, Duffy said.

Looking Ahead to Solutions

Duffy objected to a leaked draft of an unpublished report, and said the White House is completing its own study. "The president is less interested in yesterday, and more interested with today and tomorrow," he said, "so that we can be better prepared for next time."

The report puts the government response in a larger context and offers a few new details. In months of hearings, House and Senate investigative committees have already revealed the lack of White House awareness of events on the ground, political infighting between federal and state leaders, delays in ordering evacuations and the meltdown of FEMA operations.

The review suggests that federal funding be used to update state evacuation studies. It proposes making commercial airliners available in an emergency and creating a database to provide a national clearinghouse of shelter data. It also suggests naming a professional disaster adviser to the president, akin to the military's chairman of the Joint Chiefs of Staff.

U.S. disaster preparedness—individual, corporate, philanthropic and governmental—remains dangerously inadequate.

Democrats, whose leaders considered the investigation a partisan whitewash and boycotted it, called for Chertoff's removal. Reps. Charlie Melancon and William J. Jefferson, who informally participated in the inquiry, renewed calls for an independent commission styled after the one that investigated the Sept. 11 attacks, saying that the investigation, while comprehensive, was rushed, failed to compel the White House to turn over documents and held no administration officials accountable.

House investigators acknowledge that after reviewing nine hearings, scores of interviews and 500,000 pages of documents, they "will never know" what would have happened had federal, Louisiana and New Orleans officials activated plans and called on the military before the storm, and evacuated the city sooner than Aug. 28 [2005]. However, the committee found U.S. disaster preparedness—individual, corporate, philanthropic and governmental—remains dangerously inadequate.

"All the little pigs built houses of straw," it wrote. "Katrina was a national failure, an abdication of the most solemn obligation to provide for the common welfare."

Scrutinizing History's Mistakes

The report reconstructs a chronology of events over a three-week span from Aug. 22 to Sept. 12 [2005]. It focuses primarily on failures by Chertoff and the rest of the administration to execute a year-old National Response Plan and set up a related command structure, designed to marshal resources in the critical first 72 hours after a catastrophe.

The report said the single biggest federal failure was not anticipating the consequences the storm. Disaster planners had rated the flooding of New Orleans as the nation's most feared scenario, testing it under a catastrophic disaster preparedness program in 2004.

About 56 hours before Katrina made landfall, the National Weather Service and National Hurricane Center cited an "extremely high probability" that New Orleans would be flooded and tens of thousands of residents killed.

Given those warnings, the report notes Bush's televised statement on Sept. 1 [2005] that "I don't think anybody anticipated the breach of the levees," and concludes: "Comments such as those . . . do not appear to be consistent with the advice and counsel one would expect to have been provided by a senior disaster professional."

As the president's principal disaster adviser, Chertoff poorly executed many decisions, including declaring Katrina an "incident of national significance"—the highest designation under the national emergency response plan and convening an interagency board of experienced strategic advisers on Aug. 30 instead of Aug. 27, [2005] designating an untrained Brown to take charge of the disaster; and failing to invoke a federal plan that would have pushed federal help to overwhelmed state and local officials rather than waiting for them to request it.

The report said Chertoff was "confused" about Brown's role and authority, and that it was unclear why he chose him, given his lack of skills and his hostility to FEMA's downgrading under new plans.

After failing to foresee the need to muster buses, boats and aircraft, the next critical federal mistake was failure to confirm catastrophic levee breaches, the report asserts.

Despite a FEMA official's eyewitness accounts of breaches starting at 7 P.M. on Aug. 29, [2005] the president's Homeland Security Council, led by homeland security adviser Frances Fragos Townsend and her deputy, Ken Rapuano, did not consider them confirmed until 11 hours later, on Aug. 30.

The first federal order to evacuate New Orleans was not issued until 1:30 a.m. Aug. 31, and came only after FEMA's ground commander in New Orleans, Phil Parr, put out a call for buses after finding water lapping at the approaches to the Superdome, where about 12,000 victims were camped.

The city's failure to complete its mandatory evacuation . . . led to hundreds of deaths.

The council's "failure to resolve conflicts in information and the 'fog of war,' not a lack of information, caused confusion," the House panel wrote. It added that the crisis showed the government remains "woefully incapable" of managing information, much as it was before the 2001 attacks.

Spreading the Blame

The summary obtained by *The Post* generally praises pre-storm evacuations by Gulf Coast leaders, but it criticizes preparations and decisions by Louisana Gov. Kathleen Babineaux Blanco and New Orleans Mayor C. Ray Nagin, who knew that 100,000 city residents had no cars and relied on public transit. The city's failure to complete its mandatory evacuation, ordered Aug. 28, [2005] led to hundreds of deaths, the report said.

Neighboring Plaquemines Parish, by contrast, issued its order Aug. 27, helping to hold the number of storm deaths there at three. Nursing homes outside New Orleans were able to find special transportation for patients, while at least one in the city could not find bus drivers by the time people were told to leave.

The investigation also condemned "hyped media coverage of violence and lawlessness, legitimized by New Orleans authorities," for increasing security burdens, scaring away rescuers and heightening tension in the city.

It faulted Nagin for repeating, in an interview with Oprah Winfrey, rumors of armed gangs committing rapes and murder in an "almost animalistic state." The report said few cases of gunshots or violence were confirmed, although it acknowledged that few police were able to investigate and victims may have had little incentive to report crime.

11

Individuals Must Help Themselves and Each Other to Survive Disasters

Robert Tracinski

Robert Tracinski is the editor of The Intellectual Activist.

The best-laid plans and preparation made by federal, state, and local governments are ineffective if those citizens affected by disaster refuse to rely on their own initiative. People must accept personal responsibility for the protection of themselves and their families and the restoration of their property.

It took four long days for state and federal officials to figure out how to deal with the disaster in New Orleans. I can't blame them, because it also took me four long days to figure out what was going on there. The reason is that the events there make no sense if you think that we are confronting a natural disaster.

If this is just a natural disaster, the response for public officials is obvious: you bring in food, water, and doctors; you send transportation to evacuate refugees to temporary shelters; you send engineers to stop the flooding and rebuild the city's infrastructure. For journalists, natural disasters also have a familiar pattern: the heroism of ordinary people pulling together to survive; the hard work and dedication of doctors, nurses, and rescue workers; the steps being taken to clean up and rebuild.

Robert Tracinski, "An Unnatural Disaster: A Hurricane Exposes the Man-Made Disaster of the Welfare State," *The Intellectual Activist*, September 2, 2005. Reproduced by permission.

Public officials did not expect that the first thing they would have to do is to send thousands of armed troops in armored vehicle, as if they are suppressing an enemy insurgency. And journalists—myself included—did not expect that the story would not be about rain, wind, and flooding, but about rape, murder, and looting.

But this is not a natural disaster. It is a man-made disaster.

The man-made disaster is not an inadequate or incompetent response by federal relief agencies, and it was not directly caused by Hurricane Katrina. This is where just about every newspaper and television channel has gotten the story wrong.

The man-made disaster we are now witnessing in New Orleans did not happen over four days last week. It happened over the past four decades. Hurricane Katrina merely exposed it to public view.

The man-made disaster is the welfare state.

Sinking to the Occasion

For the past few days [September 2005], I have found the news from New Orleans to be confusing. People were not behaving as you would expect them to behave in an emergency— indeed, they were not behaving as they have behaved in other emergencies. That is what has shocked so many people: they have been saying that this is not what we expect from America. In fact, it is not even what we expect from a Third World country.

When confronted with a disaster, people usually rise to the occasion. They work together to rescue people in danger, and they spontaneously organize to keep order and solve problems. This is especially true in America. We are an enterprising people, used to relying on our own initiative rather than waiting around for the government to take care of us. I have seen this a hundred times, in small examples (a small town whose main traffic light had gone out, causing ordinary citizens to get out of their cars and serve as impromptu traffic cops, directing cars through the intersection) and large ones (the spontaneous response of New Yorkers to September 11).

So what explains the chaos in New Orleans?

To give you an idea of the magnitude of what is going on, here is a description from a *Washington Times* story:

"Storm victims are raped and beaten; fights erupt with flying fists, knives and guns; fires are breaking out; corpses litter the streets; and police and rescue helicopters are repeatedly fired on.

"The plea from Mayor C. Ray Nagin came even as National Guardsmen poured in to restore order and stop the looting, carjackings and gunfire. . . .

"Last night, Gov. Kathleen Babineaux Blanco said 300 Iraq-hardened Arkansas National Guard members were inside New Orleans with shoot-to-kill orders.

"'These troops are . . . under my orders to restore order in the streets,' she said. 'They have M-16s, and they are locked and loaded. These troops know how to shoot and kill and they are more than willing to do so if necessary and I expect they will.'"

The reference to Iraq is eerie. The photo that accompanies this article shows a SWAT team with rifles and armored vests riding on an armored vehicle through trash-strewn streets lined by a rabble of squalid, listless people, one of whom appears to be yelling at them. It looks exactly like a scene from Sadr City in Baghdad.

What explains bands of thugs using a natural disaster as an excuse for an orgy of looting, armed robbery, and rape? What causes unruly mobs to storm the very buses that have arrived to evacuate them, causing the drivers to speed away, frightened for their lives? What causes people to attack the doctors trying to treat patients at the Superdome?

Why are people responding to natural destruction by causing further destruction? Why are they attacking the people who are trying to help them?

My wife, Sherri, figured it out first, and she figured it out on a sense-of-life level. While watching the coverage one night on Fox News Channel, she told me that she was getting a familiar feeling. She studied architecture at the Illinois Institute of Technology, which is located in the South Side of Chicago just blocks away from the Robert Taylor Homes, one of the largest high-rise public housing projects in America. "The projects," as they were known, were infamous for uncontrollable crime and irremediable squalor. (They have since, mercifully, been demolished.)

What Sherri was getting from last night's television coverage was a whiff of the sense of life of "the projects." Then the "crawl"—the informational phrases flashed at the bottom of the screen on most news channels—have some vital statistics to confirm this sense: 75% of the residents of New Orleans had already evacuated before the hurricane, and of those who remained, a large number were from the city's public housing projects. . . .

A Sharp Contrast

There were many decent, innocent people trapped in New Orleans when the deluge hit—but they were trapped alongside large numbers of people from two groups: criminals and wards of the welfare state, people selected, over decades, for their lack of initiative and self-induced helplessness. The welfare wards were a mass of sheep, in whom the incompetent administration of New Orleans unleashed a pack of wolves.

People with values respond to a disaster by fighting against it and doing whatever it takes to overcome the difficulties they face. They don't sit around and complain that the government hasn't taken care of them.

All of this is related, incidentally, to the incompetence of the city government, which failed to plan for a total evacuation of the city, despite the knowledge that this might be necessary. In a city corrupted by the welfare state, the job of city officials is to ensure the flow of handouts to welfare recipients and patronage to political supporters—not to ensure a lawful, orderly evacuation in case of emergency.

No one has really reported this story, as far as I can tell. In fact, some are already actively distorting it, blaming President Bush, for example, for failing to personally ensure that the Mayor of New Orleans had drafted an adequate evacuation plan. The worst example is an execrable piece from the *Toronto Globe and Mail*, by a supercilious Canadian who blames the chaos on American "individualism." But the truth is precisely the opposite: the chaos was caused by a system that was the exact opposite of individualism.

The welfare state—and the brutish, uncivilized mentality it sustains and encourages—is the man-made disaster that explains the moral ugliness that has swamped New Orleans.

What Hurricane Katrina exposed was the psychological consequences of the welfare state. What we consider "normal" behavior in an emergency is behavior that is normal for people who have values and take the responsibility to pursue and protect them. People with values respond to a disaster by fighting against it and doing whatever it takes to overcome the difficulties they face. They don't sit around and complain that the government hasn't taken care of them. And they don't use the chaos of a disaster as an opportunity to prey on their fellow men.

But what about criminals and welfare parasites? Do they worry about saving their houses and property? They don't, because they don't own anything. Do they worry about what is going to happen to their businesses or how they are going to make a living? They never worried about those things before.

Do they worry about crime and looting? But living off of stolen wealth is a way of life for them.

People living in piles of their own trash, while petulantly complaining that other people aren't doing enough to take care of them and then shooting at those who come to rescue them—this is not just a description of the chaos at the Superdome. It is a perfect summary of the 40-year history of the welfare state and its public housing projects.

The welfare state—and the brutish, uncivilized mentality it sustains and encourages—is the man-made disaster that explains the moral ugliness that has swamped New Orleans. And that is the story that no one is reporting.

12

Partnerships Between Public and Private Sectors Promote Effective Recovery

Sarah Bzdega

Sarah Bzdega is a staff writer for the Business Record.

Floods, fires, tornadoes, and earthquakes can shut down a business or an entire town in a matter of minutes, and the ill-prepared risk losing everything. In the face of recent disasters, a growing number of companies are beginning to channel more time and resources into disaster planning, which also promotes a faster recovery time within their communities.

Although a near-miss by a tornado is as close as EFCO Corp. has come to a major disaster, the company's good fortune hasn't kept it from preparing for emergencies.

EFCO has been a part of Iowa Contingency Planners, an organization that provides emergency planning and disaster recovery educational and networking opportunities, since its formation in the early 1990s, and the company is in the process of updating its emergency plans.

"People here have had the attitude that says nothing is ever going to happen to us in the Midwest," said Joe Solem, legacy systems manager for EFCO and secretary of Iowa Contingency Planners. "One of these days, that's going to catch up to us."

Sarah Bzdega, "Emergency Planning a Collaborative Effort: Organizations Are Promoting Partnerships between Public and Private Sectors," *Business Record*, vol. 25, no. 5, January 29, 2007, pp. 18–19. Copyright © 2007 Business Publication Corp. Reproduced by permission.

In addition to dedicating more time and resources to disaster planning, EFCO is one of a growing number of Central Iowa companies that are joining emergency management organizations. In recent years, these groups have focused on collaborating with the public sector, and a new group, called Safeguard Iowa Partnership, is forming this year to work directly on this effort.

When a disaster strikes, businesses that are able to reopen sooner help the overall community recover sooner.

A.J. Mumm, director of emergency management for Polk County, believes businesses became proactive about putting some emergency processes in place after witnessing disasters such as the Sept. 11, 2001, terrorist attacks. More recently, these businesses also have seen a greater need to collaborate with government agencies to ensure a smoother recovery during emergency.

"The biggest thing we're finding out," Mumm said, "is that when a disaster strikes, businesses that are able to reopen sooner help the overall community recover sooner."

He added, "When the private sector owns and operates over 90 percent of the critical infrastructure we depend on, the private sector needs to be at the table with us."

Renewed Interest in Emergency Management

As more businesses recognize their need for disaster planning, emergency management groups have received renewed interest.

Last year [2006], Iowa Contingency Planners membership grew by about 17 percent to 105 members, who represent 49 companies and six government agencies. Metro Emergency Planners, composed of Greater Des Moines businesses, nearly dwindled away after Bob Goldhammer retired as Polk County's emergency management director, but has rebounded to about 70 members.

Iowa Contingency Planners' mission is to learn about and discuss certain issues businesses are facing, during quarterly meetings and an annual conference. With each member paying $100 in annual dues, Solem said the increase in membership has allowed the organization to bring in better speakers, such as Regina Phelps, an expert on pandemic planning.

"The benefit is that you're able to intermingle with peers and to keep up to date on current movements," said Tom Banse, chairman of the organization's board of directors and assistant director of business continuity, planning at Principal Financial Group Inc.

This year, Iowa Contingency Planners' theme is "Making the Connection—Partnering for Performance," which signifies its efforts to strengthen ties with government agencies. One of its major initiatives is working with Polk County emergency management officials to update the county's emergency plans, along with the Metro Emergency Planners.

Although Polk County continually revises its plans, this is one of the first times it has worked closely with the private sector, Mumm said. However, this interaction with businesses beforehand could dispel misunderstandings about what each side will do during a disaster, he said.

"We have policies and procedures in place," said Jeff McClaran, an emergency manager with Wells Fargo & Co. and chairman of the Metro Emergency Planners. "It's important for us to make sure what we have in place is going to work well with the public responders."

Metro Emergency Planners also meets quarterly to discuss different issues, which are then worked on by various committees. The organization started just after the floods of 1993 and initially was composed of downtown businesses, but now its membership has expanded to encompass all of Greater Des

Moines. Many of Iowa Contingency Planners' members belong to the organization.

One of its main objectives in working with Polk County is to develop evacuation plans to avoid situations such as traffic jams if businesses let employees leave early because of bad weather.

Building Relationships for Emergency Planning

A new group hopes to carry these initial collaborative efforts further by focusing specifically on building strong relationships between public and private emergency planners.

Already, the Safeguard Iowa Partnership [SIP] has had a strong, positive response, said Elliot Smith, executive director of the Iowa Business Council.

"As I understand it, there's been a void in getting key players from both sides together to interact and determine how procedures should be set up effectively when the time comes," Smith said. "We've had a few initial meetings with business security and disaster response experts on both sides, and the reaction has been almost overwhelming from them in terms of how much this sort of collaboration has been needed."

SIP has about 30 to 40 members from the Business Council and government agencies, but the group will formally introduce itself to the community at a Jan. 29 [2007] press conference.

Already, though, the group's members have identified some initiatives it may work on. Those include establishing an Iowa business resource registry to inventory the assets companies and state government groups have available during a crisis. It also would like to formalize representation of businesses in state emergency operations, develop better communication between the state and businesses and work on "tabletop exercises," where businesses and government entities are given a situation and together work to develop a course of action.

Coordinated Response

The group began when former Gov. Tom Vilsack met retired Air Force Gen. Charles Boyd, CEO of Business Executives for National Security [BENS], at a conference. BENS often establishes partnerships in urban areas; Smith said this is one of its first statewide programs.

The partnership is a joint effort by the Iowa Business Council and BENS. The Business Council will cover Safeguard Iowa Partnership's personnel costs up to two years, or until the organization is able to support itself. BENS is handling training and similar tasks.

Smith expects the new organization will work closely with other emergency planning groups. "We're not out to reinvent the wheel here or take the place of any existing organization," he said. "It's truly an effort to fill holes described to us by people who are experts in the area."

"It's bringing a lot of groups together and developing a coordinated and effective response at all levels."

Larger companies are encouraging smaller businesses that provide them with supplies and services to have emergency plans that will assure bigger companies that those resources will be there after a disaster.

Although larger companies, such as Principal and Wells Fargo, are leading emergency planning efforts, many smaller companies are starting to jump on board, too.

"For the past couple of decades," Mumm said, "some businesses have been able to dedicate staff and time to a specific area of continuity planning, where other small businesses can't afford to dedicate the time and personnel to do that."

However, he added, larger companies are encouraging smaller businesses that provide them with supplies and services to have emergency plans that will assure bigger companies that those resources will be there after a disaster.

Mumm said the county has tried to make the process easier by providing some basic models of emergency plans for businesses to follow.

Solem of EFCO believes it is important for every company to have some kind of emergency plan.

"We want to make sure in case of a disaster that we're able to be in business tomorrow," he said. Statistically, "the majority of companies that do not have a plan after a substantial disaster, within a couple of years are out of business."

Organizations to Contact

The editors have compiled the following list of organizations concerned with the issues debated in this book. The descriptions are derived from materials provided by the organizations. All have publications or information available for interested readers. The list was compiled on the date of publication of the present volume; the information provided here may change. Be aware that many organizations take several weeks or longer to respond to inquiries, so allow as much time as possible.

The American National Red Cross
2025 E Street NW, Washington, DC   20006
(800) 733-2767
Web site: www.redcross.org

The American Red Cross is the nation's premier emergency response organization. It offers community services to help the needy, supports military families, distributes lifesaving blood and blood products, and conducts educational programs about health and safety.

**Center for Disaster Management and
Humanitarian Assistance (CDMHA)**
13201 Bruce B. Downs Blvd., Tampa, FL   33612
(813) 974-2908 • fax: (813) 974-9980
Web site: http://cdmha.org/index.html

CDMHA is involved in education, training, and research in disaster management and humanitarian assistance. Its efforts focus on Latin America and the Caribbean.

Children's Disaster Services (CDS)
601 Main St., P.O. Box 188, New Windsor, MD   21776
(800) 451-4407 • fax: (410) 635-8739
Web site: www.brethren.org/genbd/BDM/CDSindex.html

Children's Disaster Services trains, certifies, and mobilizes volunteers to provide crisis intervention to young children of families suffering from natural or man-made disasters.

Christian Disaster Response
P.O. Box 339, Winter Haven, FL   33885
(863) 967-4357 • fax: (863) 551-1422
Web site: www.cdresponse.org

Christian Disaster Response provides disaster assistance through local churches and agencies in affected areas to provide emergency food service, home repair or rebuilding, disaster recovery supplies, and advocacy for disaster victims.

Federal Emergency Management Agency (FEMA)
500 C Street, SW, Washington, DC   20472
(800) 621-3362 • fax: (301) 362-5335
Web site: www.fema.gov

The Federal Emergency Management Agency's primary objective is to preserve lives and property, as well as protect the nation from natural disasters, man-made disasters, and acts of terrorism by leading the country in an emergency management system of preparedness, protection, mitigation, and recovery.

Friends Disaster Service, Inc.
4595 B Eliot St., Denver, CO   80211
(303) 477-1921
Web site: www.rmym.org/fds.html

Friends Disaster Service is affiliated with the National Voluntary Organizations Active in Disaster (NVOAD) and provides clean-up and rebuilding assistance to the elderly, disabled, low income, or uninsured survivors of disasters.

National Emergency Response Team (NERT)
1058 Albion Road, Unity, ME   04988
(866) 637-8872 • fax: (207) 948-3505
e-mail: bobvnert@uninets.net
Web site: www.nert-usa.org

The National Emergency Response Team meets shelter, food, and clothing needs during times of crisis and provides emergency mobile training units for temporary shelter when disasters strike.

National Organization for Victim Assistance (NOVA)
510 King St., Suite 424, Alexandria, VA   22314
(800) 879-6682
Web site: www.trynova.org

NOVA promotes rights and services for victims of crime and crisis everywhere, and sends trained crisis responders to communities traumatized by natural and man-made catastrophes.

Southern Baptist Disaster Relief
4200 North Point Parkway, Alpharetta, GA   30022
(888) 462-8657 • fax: (770) 410-6082
e-mail: dr_offisite@namb.net
Web site: www.namb.net

Southern Baptist Disaster Relief is a national network of more than 70,000 volunteers and 1,300 units that provides physical, emotional, and spiritual help to victims of natural and man-made disasters.

United States Service Command (USSC)
146 Boulder Rd., Wartburg, TN   37887
(423) 346-7697
Web site: www.usservicecommand.us

The United States Service Command establishes and maintains a volunteer organization ready to respond to assist the citizens of every community, no matter how small or large the disaster may be.

Bibliography

Books

C.V. Anderson *The Federal Emergency Management Agency*. Hauppauge, NY: Nova Science Publishers, Inc., 2003.

Bob Arnot and Mark Cohen *Your Survival: Protect Your Family and Your Home from Hurricanes, Tornadoes, Floods, Wildfires, Earthquakes, and Other Natural and Man-Made Disasters*. Long Island City, NY: Hatherleigh Press, 2007.

Thomas A. Birkland *Lessons of Disaster: Policy Changes After Catastrophic Events*. Washington, DC: Georgetown University Press, 2006.

Walter M. Brasch *Unacceptable: The Federal Response to Hurricane Katrina*. Charleston, SC: BookSurge Publishing, 2005.

Douglas Brinkley *The Great Deluge*. New York: William Morrow, 2007.

Lucien G. Canton *Emergency Management: Concepts and Strategies for Effective Programs*. Hoboken, NJ: Wiley-Interscience, 2006.

Donna Childs, Stefan Dietrich *Contingency Planning and Disaster Recovery: A Small Business Guide*. Hoboken, NJ: Wiley, 2002.

Christopher Cooper, Robert Block | *Disaster: Hurricane Katrina and the Failure of Homeland Security.* New York: Times Books, 2006.

Michael Dyson | *Come Hell or High Water: Hurricane Katrina and the Color of Disaster.* New York, NY: Basic Books, 2006.

Stephen Flynn | *The Edge of Disaster.* New York, NY: Random House, 2007.

Chester Hartman and Gregory D. Squires | *There Is No Such Thing as a Natural Disaster: Race, Class, and Hurricane Katrina.* New York, NY: Routledge, 2006.

Jed Horne | *Breach of Faith: Hurricane Katrina and the Near Death of a Great American City.* New York, NY: Random House, 2006.

Judith Kolberg | *Organize for Disaster: Prepare Your Family and Your Home for Any Natural or Unnatural Disaster.* Decatur, GA: Squall Press, 2005.

Alan M. Levitt | *Disaster Planning and Recovery: A Guide for Facility Professionals.* Hoboken, NJ: Wiley, 1997.

Barry S. Levy, Victor W. Sidel | *Terrorism and Public Health: A Balanced Approach to Strengthening Systems and Protecting People.* New York, NY: Oxford University Press. 2005.

Michael K. Lindell and Carla Prater | *Emergency Management.* Hoboken, NJ: Wiley, 2006.

K. Joanne
McGlown

Terrorism and Disaster Management: Preparing Healthcare Leaders for the New Reality. Baltimore, MD: Health Administration Press, 2004.

Charles Perrow

The Next Catastrophe: Reducing Our Vulnerabilities to Natural, Industrial, and Terrorist Disasters. Princeton, NJ: Princeton University Press, 2007.

Irwin Redlener

Americans at Risk: Why We Are Not Prepared for Megadisasters and What We Can Do. New York, NY: Knopf, 2006.

Marc Reisner

A Dangerous Place: California's Unsettling Fate. New York, NY: Pantheon Books, 2003.

David Rosner,
Gerald Markowitz

Are We Ready?: Public Health Since 9/11. Berkeley, CA: University of California Press, 2006.

Nassim Nicholas
Taleb

The Black Swan: The Impact of the Highly Improbable. New York, NY: Random House, 2007.

Periodicals

Michael Amon

"Red Cross Trains Midshipmen to Help in Disasters," *Newsday,* January 27, 2008.

Jason Burnett

"Rapid Needs Assessments for Older Adults in Disasters," *Generations,* Winter 2007.

Kathy Bushouse | "Broward County Schools Faulted for Disabled Access to Hurricane Shelters," *Sun-Sentinel*, April 27, 2008.

Sheila W. Chauvin | "In for the Long Haul," *Family & Community Health*, January–March 2008.

Susan S. Dimattia | "A Gem of a Plan: Gemological Institute of America Recovery Plan Sets Procedures for 50 Different Disasters," *Information Outlook*, June 2007.

Jamie Ellis | "Lessons Learned: The Recovery of a Research Collection after Hurricane Katrina," *Collection Building*, 2007.

Kourosh Eshghi and Richard C. Larson | "Disasters: Lessons from the Past 105 Years," *Disaster Prevention and Management*, February 2008.

David Flynn | "The Impact of Disasters on Small Business Disaster Planning," *Disasters*, December 2007.

Erica Brown Gaddis | "Full-Cost Accounting of Coastal Disaster in the United States: Implications for Planning and Preparedness," *Ecological Economics*, August 2007.

Monique Garcia and E.A. Torriero | "Midwest Earthquake a Wake-Up Call," *Chicago Tribune*, April 20, 2008.

Caron Golden | "A Tale of 3 Cities: COOP, COG and the Alphabet of 9/11," *Government Computer News*, September 11, 2006.

Tim Grant — "Have a Plan in the Event of a Disaster," *Pittsburgh Post-Gazette*, November 5, 2007.

Richard Hildreth — "Integrating Emergency and Disaster Planning," *National Civic Review*, Winter 2007.

Jeremy Olson — "State Gets High Score for Crisis Readiness: Volunteer Medical Corps Cited in Rankings," *Saint Paul Pioneer Press*, December 20, 2007.

Gretchen Parker — "Independent but Vulnerable to Disaster," *Tampa Tribune*, October 9, 2007.

John Renne — "Left Behind," *Planning*, November 2007.

Scott E. Robinson, Brian J. Gerber — "A Seat at the Table for Nondisaster Organizations," *Public Manager*, Fall 2007.

Melissa Scallan — "Colleges Work on Disaster Message Systems: Shootings Show Need for Alerts," *The Sun Herald*, February 22, 2008.

Barry Schwartz — "Imagine the Unimaginable," *Journal of Jewish Communal Service*, Fall 2007.

Matt Spetalnick — "With Katrina in Mind, Bush Views Calif. Fire Damage," *Reuters News*, October 25, 2007.

Index